WATCHING THE WAYWARD

PSALMS FOR PARENTS OF PRODIGALS

WENDY GORTON HILL

WATCHING THE WAYWARD

ENDORSEMENTS

"Wendy Gorton Hill's voice is rich and engaging. It is a healing balm for parents of prodigals. I wish my mother and father could have read Hill's poetry when I was a prodigal son." — Dr. Lyle W. Dorsett, Billy Graham Professor of Evangelism Emeritus, Beeson Divinity School. Samford University, and author of numerous books, including biographies of C. S. Lewis, E. M. Bounds, Dwight L. Moody, and Billy Sunday

"These prayers, articulated in the seemingly endless sequence of questions and the despair of waiting, [are] heart-felt and express the love of a mother's hopes and longing with a tenderness that communicates line-by-line." — Paul du Plessis, former Salvation Army physician whose own poetry can be viewed at www.thedups.com

"Lovely... honest, Christ seeking, healing. The words dance." — Sarah Suzanne Noble, poet and author of *I Cry Unto You, O Lord: Poems of Lament*

"The poems are very relatable, beautifully varied, and paired with the scripture progression... are filled with hope and sympathy. The images struck a chord!" — Karen Pommier, job coach for Safe Harbor, in Hickory, NC, helping women escape addiction and abuse

"Powerful. Very helpful for struggling parents. Many of these poems would be so helpful in worship settings." — Kyle L. White, poet and author of *Freezing, Thawing: New and Revised Stories from the Midwest*

"Profound and beautiful treasures... What a gift... with words and... the heart behind it is a treasure as well." — Nanette Helm, former teaching leader of the Westside Indianapolis Bible Study Fellowship

PRAISE FOR
"WOUNDS IN THE ENEMY'S FIELD"

"Excellent. I saw and felt it when I read it and I think many parents of prodigals will too." – Lynn Suchy, missionary to Mongolia and parent of former prodigal

"Beautiful. When we realize that we are not of this world, it brings perspective to the suffering we (and our kids) endure. I appreciate the word 'wound' because wounds heal — it speaks of hope and not defeat. Thanks for encouraging my heart." – Carol Wurtz, Salvation Army officer

"I like that these poems have a foundation in scripture. When a prodigal departs he is going into the enemy's field and all of the poems are descriptions of what happens in that field — to him and to the family." – Linda Himes, Bible teacher

TABLE OF CONTENTS

DEPARTURE

— *And he said, "There was a man who had two sons. And the younger of them said to his father, 'Father, give me the share of property that is coming to me.' And he divided his property between them. Not many days later, the younger son gathered all he had and took a journey into a far country, and there he squandered his property in reckless living.* Luke 15:11-13

Prayer for a Wayward Teen

I'm his biggest problem.
I hem him in
When he wants wings to fly.
But I can see the pig slop, Lord,
His future laid out plain.
He pictures good times;
I glimpse ruin and brokenness.
He wants our provision without our authority.
If only I could protect him, Lord.
How do you contain someone
Determined to run from you?
My arms are reaching;
My heart aching.

I know You recognize and feel my pain.
Even while You pursue us
We break Your heart.
How do You contain someone
Determined to run from You?
We beg Your blessing
Yet balk at Your boundaries
Positioned to protect us.
We think our way is best;
Our destination crystal clear to You.
We are our biggest problem.
Lord, save us from ourselves!
Turn our feet back to the path toward home.

— *Every way of a man is right in his own eyes,*
but the LORD weighs the heart. Proverbs 21:2

Residual Stench

The vacant lot beckoned both my boys.
Shoes and socks tossed aside.
Exquisite mush of mud between toes,
Delightful sensations, until the nose
Sniffed something foul.
One boy abandoned in haste.
"It smells like poo!"
The other ignored the smell
Focused only on feeling.
Finally, it overpowered even him.
After hosing down,
A shower,
And a good long scrub,
The stench lingered.
Lord, why can some dance in the dirt,
Then dash away,
While others remain to play
Too long?
Consequences cling.
The stench suffocating.
Depth of danger undetected
Until too late.
For one, a sip,
Another, a chain.
And even if You break the bonds,
The tell-tale marks may yet remain.

— *Be sure your sin will find you out.* Numbers 32:23b

Wounds in the Enemy's Field

We walk in the wake of his devastation,
The trail of his perilous, prodigal way,
Knee-deep in wreckage and ruination,
Following footsteps that stumble and stray.

His tread detonates with reverberations,
Spilling on others with astonishing speed,
Riddled with radical ramifications,
Driven by constant and insatiable need.

Everyone's touched by his traumatization,
Unexpected upheaval that alters life.
The enemy's plan? Incapacitation,
Triggering explosions of conflict and strife.

He wends unaware of annihilation,
Uncomprehending what the surface may hide.
He seeks his solace in intoxication.
We cannot dodge landmines without You as guide.

So hear our humble and patient petition,
Protect us from wounds in the enemy's field,
Inspire within us a deep-felt contrition,
Disable the tripwires that Satan may wield.

—*The thief comes only to steal and kill and destroy.* John 10:10a

Who's the Prodigal?

I am just as guilty
Of wanting my own way;
I fail just as often
To submit and to obey.
I rebel against Your rule.
I dictate my desires.
I fail to see the promise
In Your refining fires.
I need Your guiding hand
Every bit as much;
Oh, please, be patient, Lord,
Redirect me with Your touch.

— *Then Jesus said to his disciples, "If any of you wants to be my follower, you must give up your own way, take up your cross, and follow me.* Matthew 16:24 (NLT)

Runaway Train

He was safely headed on straight tracks
Until the drug's introduction
Switched him onto
An unintended side rail.
Now, as he accelerates toward certain destruction,
Unaware he has been diverted,
We know he's gone off-course.
Powerless on the sidelines,
We dread the impending train wreck,
Wondering what damages he will incur.
Unable to block his path
Or deter this looming disaster,
We bear signs, desperately trying to alert him.
"Slow down!"
"Stop!"
"The bridge is out!"
But the wheels roll on, hugging the rails.
We know nothing about the approaching gap.
Is it over low land or on a bridge over a ravine?
Will his crash bring minimal casualties
Or will he plunge to utter annihilation?
Lord, he may hurtle out-of-control,
Filling our lives with uncertainty,
But You remain in control, our only hope.
You provide supernatural peace
In the midst of chaos.
We beg You to lay down trap points
That will safely derail him onto a sandbar,
Fending off further harm.

Lord, bring him home
Before he crashes and burns.

— Do not be anxious about anything, but in everything by prayer and supplication with thanksgiving let your requests be made known to God. Philippians 4:6

Lying With the Dogs

Yesterday,
One picked a fight,
Distracting him
While another stole his bag.
Yet we couldn't call
The defenders of justice
For fear of what he carried.
What was lost is unimportant
Compared to what he might gain.
You can use this as a tool.
Give him understanding, Lord.
His choice of company
Determines his character.
Open his eyes to see
That wicked friends
Will only lead
To evil ends.

— *The righteous choose their friends carefully, but the way of the wicked leads them astray.* Proverbs 12:26 (NIV)

Clouded Perspective

In his eyes, I'm wrong, Lord.

My views are invalid;

My stance unsound.

He is astonished

That I cannot see

The desirability of his diversions,

The advantage of his actions.

His vision is blurred.

Wrong is right;

Right is wrong.

What is illegal

Should be permitted.

He thinks I only balk

Because I'm too uptight,

Too straight-laced

To break boundaries,

To reject rules.

Lord, correct his vision.

Help him to see

He's chosen a path

That leads to pain.

Open his eyes

To the waste in which he wallows,

To the slop he gladly swallows.

May he abandon his activities,

May his feet fly for home,

Where I am waiting,

Eyes brimming with tears,

Arms aching with emptiness,
Heart seizing with hope.

— Woe to those who call evil good and good evil, who put darkness for light and light for darkness, who put bitter for sweet and sweet for bitter! Woe to those who are wise in their own eyes, and shrewd in their own sight! Isaiah 5:20-21

DISCIPLINE

— And when he had spent everything, a severe famine arose in that country, and he began to be in need. So he went and hired himself out to one of the citizens of that country, who sent him into his fields to feed pigs. And he was longing to be fed with the pods that the pigs ate, and no one gave him anything. Luke 15:14-16

Double-minded

I give it
Then I grab it back.
I rest
Then my heart races.
Like a yo-yo,
Up
And
Down,
Trusting
Then despairing.
Your hands so capable;
Mine so clumsy.
Fear fights faith.
Doubt destroys dependence,
And vice versa.
Oh, for steadfastness
When waves crash
When waters rise
When tempests threaten
I lift my eyes
And see You—
Feel in Your hand
All the strength I need
To stand.

— Let us hold fast to the confession of our hope without wavering, for he who promised is faithful. Hebrews 10:23

Baggage Complicates

I think my husband's too soft.
His father hole leaves him
Desperate for closeness
Rather than discipline.
In my eyes, he enables.
He thinks I'm too strict.
My tight-laced upbringing lends a
Desire for rules and order
Rather than relationship.
In his eyes, I alienate.
Lord, we're butting heads.
The friction foments.
We desperately need unity
But the enemy pulls us apart,
Preying on our weaknesses,
Appealing to our vulnerabilities.
He wins when we divide.
Lord, we both want the same thing—
Our child's return to right relationship
With us and with You.
If I didn't ache for his restitution
I wouldn't care what path we choose.
But this matters, Lord!
It could be life or death.
So much rides on what we do.
Yet, there's the rub—
The outcome doesn't depend on us.
You have it all in hand.
You neither enable nor alienate.

You gently draw.

You lovingly accept.

How is Your way both strict and soft,

Both commanding and compelling?

You carefully balance justice and grace.

Remind us to lay it all in Your hands

And give us a united front of wisdom and diplomacy.

Where Satan would divide us, Lord, bring us together.

He's my ally, not my enemy.

I'm his partner, not his foe.

Let us set aside the baggage and cooperate—

United in our goal.

— I appeal to you, brothers, by the name of our Lord Jesus Christ, that all of you agree, and that there be no divisions among you, but that you be united in the same mind and the same judgment. 1 Corinthians 1:10

Frequent Flyer on If Only Airlines

If only… he hadn't broken his leg in the season's first game, shattering his identity.

If only… they hadn't prescribed pain pills insufficient to meet his desperate need.

If only… a friend hadn't offered an alternative that enticed and intoxicated.

If only… football friends hadn't abandoned him, leaving him to seek new friends.

If only… the drug group hadn't welcomed him so graciously and eagerly.

If only… he hadn't been genetically predisposed to addiction.

If only… we'd identified his needs better and sought to meet them more effectively.

If only… strong Christian friends could have reined him back in when he began to stray.

But what might have been is not what was.

You were not confounded, startled, unaware.

You knew, before time began, where this story would wend and weave.

You allowed this pain into our lives with purpose and precision.

If only… does me no good.

Our ways didn't slip beneath Your radar.

You gave the inheritance knowing full well

It would be squandered and we would come up empty.

Only if… we return to You will we cease to stray.

Only if… we see our desperate need of You will we seek You as our source.

Only if… we place our propensities in Your hands can You use them profitably.

Only if… we rely on You can we graciously and patiently await our child's return.

Only if… we recognize our identity as Your child will we run to You as Father.

Only if… we come up empty will we ask to be more fully filled.

Only if… every alternative fails, will we realize Your sufficiency.

Only if… You break us, can the light shine through, revealing You.

— *For godly grief produces a repentance that leads to salvation without regret, whereas worldly grief produces death.* 2 Corinthians 7:10

When Ignorance Ignites Imagination

Too many times, I'm out of my mind
Wondering who, what, and where?
What is he doing? Where is he going?
What will the consequences bear?
Possibilities pour over me like a tsunami—
Thoughts in high gear.
>Trouble with the law?
>Incarceration?
>With his health?
>Hospitalization?
Looking behind I sadly find
Reason to fear.
>School expulsion,
>Lungs that are damaged,
>Four-day fever,
>Lymph nodes enlarged.
I feel too sure there's more to endure;
I cannot see the future clearly.
Will he join the thugs doing harder drugs?
I need Your hope so dearly.
Instead I dread what lies ahead.
Can we take much more?
The questions ignite a hideous fright—
We have no idea what's in store.
If a crystal ball could see it all,
Would I really want to know?
You are right to limit the light
On a future tumbling domino.
My imagination only fuels agitation;

Please temper the thoughts in my brain.
I senselessly grope for any kind of hope,
A calm inside this hurricane.
So give me grace in this hesitant place.
Let me rest in Your guarantee—
I should have known we're not alone.
You are with him and with me.
Looking ahead I have nothing to dread
Because You promise to remain.
You will direct; You will protect;
You will, in all things, sustain.
I give You my tears, these imagined fears;
I rest in Your sovereignty.
Shift my eyes to actualize
Your vast possibility.
So with him, go, where I cannot go,
Be with him while we're apart,
Hold me, Lord, in Your Word
And calm my anxious heart.
Remind me to climb one step at a time,
And leave tomorrow to You.
This tense dance is just a chance
For You to see us through.

—*He is not afraid of bad news; his heart is firm, trusting in the LORD.*
Psalm 112:7

"Worry does not empty tomorrow of its sorrow. It empties today of its strength." — Corrie Ten Boom

The Divine Alchemist

"Alchemist: Someone who transforms things for the better"
— *Merriam-Webster*

I carry heavy burdens,
Beyond what I can bear;
I cry out in agony,
Crave Your tender touch there,
For You turn each common thing
To trials laced with gold.
Looking back upon my life
Rich blessings I behold.

Moving in my senior year
Seemed the ultimate end,
Isolated and alone,
Without a single friend.
Yet You transformed me there—
Such an education;
I began to recognize
My flimsy foundation.
Friends, church, and activities
Would never see me through;
What I truly needed then
Was simply more of You.

Marital separation—
A hefty load to carry.
Who anticipates the trials
When they set out to marry?
I thought it would shatter us,

Our marriage, almost dead.
The future bleak, uncertain,
Our hearts consumed with dread.
Yet You knit us back together
In ways we couldn't have dreamed;
Strengthened by the trial,
Our relationship redeemed.

So as my shoulders sag beneath
My current leaden load,
I choose to lift my eyes from
My footsteps on the road.
Experience has taught me
You gift amid the pain,
Blessings of understanding,
Loss brings about great gain.
You shape us and You shield us,
You weave our stories long,
Till every thorn and thistle
Prods an unexpected song.

— *He will sit like a refiner of silver, burning away the dross. He will purify the Levites, refining them like gold and silver, so that they may once again offer acceptable sacrifices to the LORD.* Malachi 3:3 (NLT)

Chisel Me

This child of mine
Opens avenues unexplored,
Reveals inadequacies unrecognized,
Exposes vulnerabilities once hidden,
Unveils the true measure of the man,
In darkest moments
Teaches me to trust,
In proud moments
Stirs my heart to song.
I am his teacher,
Yet he teaches me, Lord.
As I seek to shape him,
So You sharpen me.
Work with this child
To mold me, Your child.

— *Let us test and examine our ways, and return to the LORD!*
Lamentations 3:40

When Comparison Steals My Joy

I'm trusting, Lord,

Hanging by a thread;

Then I open social media

To accolades, achievements,

Proclamations of parental pride

And my heart shrivels.

Satan swirls in and sucks away my fortitude.

Why aren't they called to carry my burdens, Lord?

Did they earn their child's good fortune?

Did I earn my child's rebellion?

Your rain falls without explanation or justification.

You needn't defend Yourself to me,

Your way is best, I know.

Still, that niggling comparison thief sneaks in.

I hold my tears of terror

Next to their songs of success

And it feels unfair.

Who decides fair? Not me.

I am the elder brother envious of

The celebration thrown for someone else.

There is gift in my battle,

Just as there may be pain hiding within their joy,

Pain they don't express, but

You discipline, You develop each of us.

It cannot all be roses. Remind me of that.

When my finger pricks upon the thorn, spilling blood,

Let me focus on the beauty of the flower.

— But who are you, O man, to answer back to God? Will what is molded say to its molder, "Why have you made me like this?" Romans 9:20

Distracted by Other Runners

I run this life race alongside fitter folk.
They are swift-footed,
Blessed with grace and strength
And forceful limbs well-cut for running,
While I seem confined to a body that betrays me,
My limbs weak and disfigured,
Not beautiful like theirs,
My strides disjointed,
Not graceful like theirs,
My breathing ragged and uneven.
I want their limbs, their strides, their air.
I too could run like that
If I hadn't these burdens and afflictions, Lord.
You gently remind
"Focus on the road before you
Rather than the runner beside you!"
And when I cut through that finish line,
Oh, sweet joy,
Hard-fought victory,
Sweeter success.
You will adorn my neck with ribbons of glory
To recognize the amazing achievement.
But in the meantime, as I raggedly run,
Excise my envy, Lord.
Give my wobbly legs strength enough for every step.

— *Let your eyes look directly forward, and your gaze be straight before you.*
Proverbs 4:25

"I think He receives more glory through limping people who are dependent on Him, than healthy people who breeze through life independent of Him." — Sue Bohlin — https://blogs.bible.org/a-holy-limp/

Clenched Hands

Amid chaos, I plead, "Lord, don't You see;
This cannot be what You have planned for me."
My unbelief assumes You have gone wrong.
Like my rebelling son, I am too headstrong.
When I come to You, my fists are clenched tight,
Sure my situation is an oversight.
Clutching my plans and my sense of control,
A foolish child, pushing against Your role.
Lord, open my hands, pry each finger wide,
Forgive the affront of inflated pride
That presumes I know best when I know squat.
You reign supreme; help me trust as I ought.
I lift outstretched hands and take what You give,
Open to Your will, My doubts, please forgive.

— Immediately the father of the child cried out and said, "I believe; help my unbelief!" Mark 9:24

"When I was sure that the Lord had forgotten me… I heard the Holy Spirit whisper in my ear… 'You are not so important, nor so complicated, that you will be God's first mistake.'" — Mary Dorsett

While on the Wheel

I'm a masterpiece
Held in Your capable hand,
Lovingly chiseled
In ways I don't understand.
Remind me, again,
Of the purpose in the pain;
You craft vast beauty,
Magnificence from mundane.
I praise Your pressure,
Prize Your moments of restraint,
Hail Your shrewd handling,
Fight every careless complaint.
As clay in Your hands
I submit to Your desire,
Knowing redemption
Follows Your refining fire.

— *But now, O LORD, you are our Father; we are the clay, and you are our potter; we are all the work of your hand.* Isaiah 64:8

"Like a skilled potter, He knows how to apply precise pressure, when to relax His grip, how to score our life with His fingernail, how to squeeze and nudge—all of which increases our fitness as a vessel for His use. At times the Master Potter places us in the kiln where the fires of life turn us into stronger vessels." — David Jeremiah — https://davidjeremiah.blog/what-it-means-to-be-clay-in-the-hands-of-the-potter/

DISILLUSIONMENT

— But when he came to himself, he said, "How many of my father's hired servants have more than enough bread, but I perish here with hunger! I will arise and go to my father, and I will say to him, 'Father, I have sinned against heaven and before you. I am no longer worthy to be called your son. Treat me as one of your hired servants.'" — Luke 15:17-19

Only You Fit

He has a hole
Made for You,
Yet, he fills it with
Friends,
Feelings,
Drugs,
Unrealistic expectations,
Insufficient substitutions.
Unveil his hollow hopes,
Shine Your light
Where darkness deceives.
Kick the flimsy supports
Out from under him.
Reveal his unstable foundation.
He has given his heart
To the way of the world,
But friends can be false,
Feelings fickle,
And drugs disarming.
He remains
Enchanted,
Beguiled,
Persuaded his prescription
Will pacify the pain
Only You can penetrate.
Intensify his ache.
Identify Your answer.
Clarify his scarcity.
Confirm Your sufficiency.

Give him eyes to see

Through the deception

To Your truth

Until he seeks

The only source

That truly satisfies.

— *Enter by the narrow gate. For the gate is wide and the way is easy that leads to destruction, and those who enter by it are many. For the gate is narrow and the way is hard that leads to life, and those who find it are few.* — Matthew 7:13-14

"Thou hast made us for Thyself, O Lord, and our hearts are restless until they rest in Thee." — St. Augustine, *Confessions*

"If I find in myself a desire which no experience in this world can satisfy, the most probable explanation is that I was made for another world." — C. S. Lewis, *Mere Christianity*

Yearning for Yesterday

"Nostalgia: A wistful or excessively sentimental yearning for return to or of some past period or irrecoverable condition" — *Merriam-Webster*

"Hiraeth: Welsh term for a homesickness for a home to which you cannot return, a home which maybe never was; the nostalgia, the yearning, the grief for the lost places of your past." — Google Images

I'm drawn by pictures
Of him as a boy,
Earlier chapters
Bursting with joy,
Pages of time
We cannot retrieve,
Our current darkness
We didn't conceive.
The ache, the longing,
For days gone past,
Purity ruptured,
It did not last.
The brightness of
His smiling face.
He left the safety
Of that secure place.
That smile gave way
To a caustic smirk,
To a demeanor
Certain to irk.
I almost wanted
To take them down;
They summoned sorrow,

Invoked a frown.
Pictures were painful,
Memories revealed
Innocence stolen
On this battlefield.
We cannot go back,
Eden is lost,
He chose to depart,
A line was crossed.
Help us to live
In this land of sin,
Not looking back
To where and when
But gazing forward
To what You will do
When You take the old
And make it new.
Freedom forfeited
With just one bite;
Give strength to press on
Till You make it right.

— Say not, "Why were the former days better than these?" For it is not from wisdom that you ask this. Ecclesiastes 7:10

Send Him a Nathan

It's clear he won't hear our voices;
Our pressures don't change his choices.
Parental pull fails every time;
Arguments dull, he sees no crime.
His eyes are blind, his way unclear,
He doesn't mind, nor does he fear;
His way looks best in his own eyes.
Despite unrest he buys the lies.
The enemy, subtle and keen,
With trickery remains unseen.
What will it take to draw him back?
So much at stake, yet pull we lack.

Perhaps he needs a Nathan, Lord,
A voice whose pleads won't be ignored.
Bring him a friend, who doubts his path,
Who says the end will lead to wrath,
Offering truth he will not hear,
Esteemed youth who bends his ear
Saying what we cannot express.
To make him see his vain excess.
A Nathan, Lord, who can ideally
Easily afford to prod freely.
One he respects and will regard
Who can reflect a view that's hard.

My heart is sick from hope deferred.
You could heal quick, with just one word;
If not from You, then from a friend
Who will get through and recommend

A clear-cut way to get back home,

To end the fray, and cease to roam.

Back in Your arms, drugs left behind,

Away from harms that tempt and bind,

He then might see our point of view.

I guarantee we will praise You

For sending one to reel him in

And lure our son back from his sin.

— *My brothers, if anyone among you wanders from the truth and someone brings him back, let him know that whoever brings back a sinner from his wandering will save his soul from death and will cover a multitude of sins.* James 5:19-20

— In 2 Samuel 1:1-25, when King David committed adultery with Bathsheba, sent her husband to the front line of battle to certain death in order to cover his sin, and then married Bathsheba, the Lord sent the prophet Nathan to David. His words opened the king's eyes to the sin he had committed. Nathan's rebuke led to David's repentance and opened the way to God's restoration.

Shatter Satan's Strongholds

Discovered further evidence today
Of Satan's tricky power and his sway.
He woos my son with promises of highs
And pulls him under dangerous riptides.
Those currents seem to grip and overwhelm.
Unwittingly, he yields to Satan's realm,
While I stand on the shore frozen with fear
Afraid I'll see him slowly disappear.
I cannot rescue my son from the deep;
The chasm is too wide, the waves too steep.
But I know that You have made the water
And I'm confident You see Your daughter
Weeping, wailing, and begging for Your hand
To pull this son, at last, onto dry land.
We suffocate beneath our sin and fear.
We need to know that You will yet be near,
Ready to throw us a life preserver,
A witness to the random observer—
Who is certain the outcome will be grave—
That You, alone, can span the deep and save.

— And they may come to their senses and escape from the snare of the devil, after being captured by him to do his will. 2 Timothy 2:26

"The 'deceiver' uses specific, subtle, stealthy plans to target each individual, his goal being to defeat, discourage and dishearten. Stated another way, Satan's attacks are 'tailor made' ('the schemes'), carefully and methodically selected to attack each person's specific weaknesses and vulnerabilities. His wiles and methods are usually attractive, always deceptive, and often ensnaring." — from an excellent, though lengthy, article outlining the schemes of the devil: https://www.preceptaustin.org/schemes-of-the-devil

When I Fear the Water

As a parent, Lord, I know
That water equals danger.
If my child must be near it,
I don't want him to fear it.
He needs to work with water,
Approaching it with wisdom,
Understanding how to swim
In case he ever falls in.
Yet, I relate to his dread
When he's thrown in unprepared.
I know his courage will shrink
When he thinks that he might sink.
I offer encouragement:
"Flap your arms to keep you up."
"If you lay flat as a boat,
You'll discover you can float."
Yet, when I look in his eyes,
I recognize his terror,
That sinking thought when I must
Brave the deep in total trust.
You encourage me again
To rely wholly on You.
When raging waters surround,
Resting in You, I have found
I can flap arms of faith,
I can float in Your care.
The water will not threaten
Despite the fears that set in.
So, when tossed in deep water,

Help me understand Your plan.

For thy test is for my best

If I learn to truly rest.

— Count it all joy, my brothers, when you meet trials of various kinds, for you know that the testing of your faith produces steadfastness. And let steadfastness have its full effect, that you may be perfect and complete, lacking in nothing. James 1:2-4

"We are not necessarily doubting that God will do the best for us; we are wondering how painful the best will turn out to be." — C. S. Lewis

Revive My Heart

I'm worn out, Lord.
Beaten,
Battered,
Bruised,
Weary of this war
And the fear that we might
Lose.
He is so intent
On going his
Own way.
I can do
Nothing
But pray.
I am fatigued, Lord.
Helpless,
Harried,
Heartsick,
Satan's darts and arrows
Come on
Thick.
Frazzled by the fears,
The endless, quenchless
Tears,
Worried that this path
May weave
For many
Years.
I am out of gas, Lord.
Drained,

Discouraged,
Debilitated,
If he would
Shift a bit,
I would be elated.
When all my
Strength is gone
And I cannot lift
My sword,
I lean upon
Your promises
And open up
Your Word.
The battle is not
Mine to win;
You've already
Conquered death and sin.
When deeply dismayed,
My faith forlorn,
You remind me
It can be borne,
Not in my power
To supersede,
To push my way,
To meet my need,
But in submission
To Your will,
Knowing You can
Conquer still,
And draw him home
When I cannot,

To still my fears

When I'm distraught.

So, I am trusting, Lord.

Enabled,

Encouraged,

Energized,

Now I recognize,

I need not

Feel paralyzed.

When my knees

Are weak,

I need only

Stand,

Watch Your amazing power,

View Your triumphant hand.

— He gives power to the faint, and to him who has no might he increases strength. Isaiah 40:29

Dancing With the Worst-case Scenario

When the worst-case scenario
Pulls me into a two-step,
Life begins a counterclockwise sway.
Quick steps with assumptions,
Slow steps with possibilities,
He changes my direction
As I follow his lead.
Endless fears cause
My heart to weave,
My mind to whirl,
Winding and unwinding,
Threading arms with
What might happen.
He proposes so many
Pivots and turns
I'm dizzy with dread.
So, I beg You, Lord,
Pull me from this partner,
Break in on this dance,
Still my heart and mind.
I'll follow Your lead,
Safe in Your arms,
Resting in the rhythm
Of Your control.
No longer swept
Into his tales of woe.

— *Therefore do not be anxious about tomorrow, for tomorrow will be anxious for itself. Sufficient for the day is its own trouble.* Matthew 6:34

"Never be afraid to trust an unknown future to a known God." — Corrie Ten Boom

RETURN

— And he arose and came to his father. But while he was still a long way off, his father saw him and felt compassion, and ran and embraced him and kissed him. And the son said to him, "Father, I have sinned against heaven and before you. I am no longer worthy to be called your son." Luke 15:20-21

I Know Your Extravagant Grace

I've walked his road,
His path is familiar,
My story is one
Of a prodigal, too.
As my steps strayed,
I remained unaware,
The distance I put
Between me and You.
I doubted You,
Distrusted Your love,
Sure that I knew
What would satisfy.
I was deceived,
My selfish endeavor,
Never able
To fully gratify.
Yet You waited—
Waited with open arms—
For me to repent
And return to the fold.
I came back home
To Your loving embrace,
Weary of the
Chasm and the cold.
Now I'm the one
Receiving rebellion.
Remind me of
That difficult place—
Alone, apart,

Aware of what is lost—
In need of Your
Extravagant grace.
Help me, like You,
To grant understanding,
To recognize
The wending of our ways,
To offer love
Despite his detachment,
Ignoring the
Pain of all his delays.
So bring him back,
I am waiting, too,
To feel him rest
Again within my arms.
Open his eyes
And open his ears,
To see and hear
The desperate alarms.
You called me back,
Now beckon him, too,
Summon him with
The standard he spurns.
And I will trust
Entirely on You;
All praise be Yours
When he, at last, returns.

— All we like sheep have gone astray; we have turned—every one—to his own way; and the LORD has laid on him the iniquity of us all. Isaiah 53:6

Remind Me of the Morning

In the night,

Dark is a shroud,

Death a foregone conclusion.

It appears

Everything

Will constantly lead

To decay and demise,

Every step

Feels disastrous,

Laced with anxiety,

Charged with conflict,

Saturated with sorrow.

Satan urges

"Give up hope!

Embrace despair!"

Remind me, then—

That night gives way

To morning.

Kindle hope

And fires

Of persistent prayer,

Dish out discipline,

Restore life.

Even if the end

Isn't what I'd imagined

And the night seems long,

I cling to You

Because joy

Comes in the morning.

— I will extol you, O LORD, for you have drawn me up and have not let my foes rejoice over me. O LORD my God, I cried to you for help, and you have healed me. O LORD, you have brought up my soul from Sheol; you restored me to life from among those who go down to the pit. Sing praises to the LORD, O you his saints, and give thanks to his holy name. For his anger is but for a moment, and his favor is for a lifetime. Weeping may tarry for the night, but joy comes with the morning. Psalm 30:1-5

Revive

He chooses a life of death.

How can it be so alluring?

Doesn't he see his way is securing

A corpse—a dead man?

It rots his brain, it saps his soul,

It leaves him empty, less than whole,

Yet all the while he says he's fine.

He thinks his "medicine" meets a need,

Oh, God, we beg You to intercede.

Bring him to the end of himself.

Hear our cries, our anguished moans,

Then, breathe life into his bones.

Make him a testimony,

A picture of Your regeneration,

The triumph of Your sweet salvation.

— *Thus says the Lord GOD to these bones: Behold, I will cause breath to enter you, and you shall live. And I will lay sinews upon you, and will cause flesh to come upon you, and cover you with skin, and put breath in you, and you shall live, and you shall know that I am the LORD." // Then he said to me, "Son of man, these bones are the whole house of Israel. Behold, they say, 'Our bones are dried up, and our hope is lost; we are indeed cut off.' Therefore prophesy, and say to them, 'Thus says the Lord GOD: Behold, I will open your graves and raise you from your graves, O my people. And I will bring you into the land of Israel. And you shall know that I am the LORD, when I open your graves, and raise you from your graves, O my people. And I will put my Spirit within you, and you shall live, and I will place you in your own land. Then you shall know that I am the LORD; I have spoken, and I will do it, declares the LORD.'"* Ezekiel 37:5-6, 11-14

Carving a Path to Peace Through Praise

How I crave peace
Amid frantic days.
You have declared
The path to peace is praise.
So I praise You for Your constant love
When human love feels conditional.
I praise You for Your guidance
When we cannot see our way.
I praise You for Your reconciliation
When the chasm seems colossal.
I praise You for beauty
When the world turns ugly.
I praise You for grace
When we rightly deserve death.
I praise You for salvation
When we're sinking in sin.
I praise You for Your patience
When we cannot hold it together.
I praise You for Your accessibility;
When we pray You always hear.
I praise You for Your sovereignty
When our plans are frustrated.
I praise You for keeping Your promises
When we so often break ours.
I praise You for pursuing us
When we go our own way.
I praise You for forgiving us
When we repent and turn to You.
I praise You for Your omnipotence

When it feels like evil will win.

I praise You for Your omniscience

When we think our way is hidden.

I praise You for Your omnipresence

When we feel we are alone.

With sickle of praise

I prune back the weeds

Of noise and distress;

My worry recedes.

— *Do not be anxious about anything, but in everything by prayer and supplication with thanksgiving let your requests be made known to God. And the peace of God, which surpasses all understanding, will guard your hearts and your minds in Christ Jesus. Finally, brothers, whatever is true, whatever is honorable, whatever is just, whatever is pure, whatever is lovely, whatever is commendable, if there is any excellence, if there is anything worthy of praise, think about these things. What you have learned and received and heard and seen in me—practice these things, and the God of peace will be with you.* Philippians 4:6-9

"We would worry less if we praised more. Thanksgiving is the enemy of discontent and dissatisfaction." — Harry Ironside

Progression to Enemy Flight

I

Must identify

Who and *how*

To attack.

I am fighting *not my son*

But *spiritual forces of darkness*

Intent upon claiming him for their own.

Satan aims to leave me

Defeated

Discouraged

Doubtful

Frustrated

Hopeless

But I have vast weapons

To wield against him.

The armor of God:

Truth to fight his deception

Righteousness against his evil

The *Gospel of Peace* to fight discouragement

Faith against the doubts

Salvation for assurance of my identity

And the powerful *Word of God,*

A two-edged sword revealing the

Full intent of the heart.

The outcome is sure.

God's power trumps Satan's

Every time.

With God, one can route a thousand.

With God, I send the enemy
Fleeing *seven* different ways.

— *The LORD will cause your enemies who rise against you to be defeated before you. They shall come out against you one way and flee before you seven ways.* Deuteronomy 28:7

Fortify My Response

Lord, make me a Churchill

When I want to go AWOL,

When the battle intensifies

Beyond what I feel I can bear,

When all around seems

Dark and foreboding,

When an end is not in sight,

Gird me up.

Make me strong and courageous.

Not a Pollyanna, no—

Not minimizing the gravity

Of the battle before me—

But, instead, in my candor

About the conflict,

Let me communicate courage

And fearlessness.

Confident, not in my ability

To withstand the storm,

But in Your ability to

Calm the waves,

Fight the fray,

Defeat the enemy,

And conquer darkness.

Help me to persevere

With fortitude

So that I might

Never,

Never,

Never

Give up.

— But we are not of those who shrink back and are destroyed, but of those who have faith and preserve their souls. Hebrews 10:39

Tenuous Calm

He hasn't used in months.
Hope limps in on crutches while
Suspicion lingers in the shadows.
What keeps him clean for now
May disappear tomorrow.
Dare I trust this calm, Lord?
Has he turned a corner?
Or will my dreams be dashed
When what supports him now
Slips out from beneath him
In a crushing fall?
Anything could trigger relapse—
Stress,
Friends,
Disappointment,
Opportunity—
Remind me
Where my hope comes from.
It is in You,
Not in circumstances.
Hold each of us close—
Him and me—
Send suspicion packing.
You have a
Purpose and plan.
Guide and guard.
Thank You for every
Moment of tranquility
On this long-winding path.

— Be strong, and let your heart take courage, all you who wait for the LORD! Psalm 31:24

"I don't know what the future may hold, but I know who holds the future."
— Ralph Abernathy

Protected by Your Pinions

"Pinion: n. 1. The end joint of a bird's wing 2. A wing 3. Any wing feather"
— *Webster's New World Dictionary*

"Once (Psalm 91:4) it stands in a figurative expression for the protective care of Yahweh, which is bestowed on those who trust in Him."
— *International Standard Bible Encyclopedia*

I trust in You.
I nestle 'neath
Your pinions.
Covered,
Sheltered,
Safe in Your care,
Shielded from danger,
I rest in the shadow of
Your wings.
I burrow beneath
Your fierce feathers.
Trusting,
Nestling,
Resting,
Burrowing,
You are my refuge.
Your pinions protect
Me and my prodigal.

— *He will cover you with his pinions, and under his wings you will find refuge; his faithfulness is a shield and buckler.* Psalm 91:4

— *Be merciful to me, O God, be merciful to me, for in you my soul takes refuge; in the shadow of your wings I will take refuge, till the storms of destruction pass by.* Psalm 57:1

You Steer; I'm Just a Pinion

"Pinion: n. A small cogwheel the teeth of which fit into those of a larger gearwheel or those of a rack" — *Webster's New World Dictionary*

A rack and pinion is used to steer a car or to move a train up a steep incline.

Let me be one small gear
In the process of moving
My prodigal home.
I want to follow
Your lead.
Help me to mesh with
Your patterns,
Your plans,
Your purpose.
If by
My prayer,
My fasting,
My submission,
I may play a small part,
I will be well pleased.

— I will instruct you and teach you in the way that you should go; I will counsel you with my eye upon you. Psalm 32:8

When Satan Seeks to Pinion

"Pinion: vt. 1. To cut off or bind the pinions of (a bird) to keep it from flying 2. To bind (the wings) 3. To disable or impede by binding the arms of 4. To confine or shackle" — *Webster's New World Dictionary*

Satan's goal is bondage.
With malicious intent
He holds my child back
From God-given potential.
He seeks through
False perceptions of freedom—
Intensely demanded autonomy—
To bind and control.
When it seems my son
Is bound fast in chains,
Shackled to addictions,
Voracious needs,
I run to You
Because only in submission
To You
Do we gain full freedom.
As my child's plea for independence
Leads to slavery,
So my cry of dependence
On You
Leads to liberty.
Help my son
Recognize this paradox.
Release him from
Satan's pinioning persuasion.
Return him to Your nest.

— *They promise them freedom, but they themselves are slaves of corruption. For whatever overcomes a person, to that he is enslaved.* 2 Peter 2:19

— *For the law of the Spirit of life has set you free in Christ Jesus from the law of sin and death. // that the creation itself will be set free from its bondage to corruption and obtain the freedom of the glory of the children of God.* Romans 8:2, 21

REJOICING

— But the father said to his servants, "Bring quickly the best robe, and put it on him, and put a ring on his hand, and shoes on his feet. And bring the fatted calf and kill it, and let us eat and celebrate. For this my son was dead, and is alive again; he was lost, and is found. Luke 15:22-24

Hide and Seek

Are You hiding, Lord?

I am hunting.

Looking

Over,

Under,

Around.

Sometimes it seems

You've left the building.

All is silent.

Nothing moves.

Nothing shifts

In my muddled world.

Wait!

I see You

In the silence,

In the muddle.

You are waiting

As I'm waiting.

You are seeking

As I seek.

You see me as I am.

I now see You

As You are.

More than just a game,

I find great value

In seeking and finding

You.

Unhidden,

Unbidden,

Ever true!

— She gave this name to the LORD who spoke to her: "You are the God who sees me," for she said, "I have now seen the One who sees me." Genesis 16:13 (NIV)

Altered Vision

Lord, shift my perspective to Your own
To recognize the purpose in Your plan.
What seems an affliction, may be an avenue;
What seems a blight, may be a blessing.
Every harm reveals Your help;
Every grief contains Your gift.
Within the problem, hides a promise;
Within the ordeal, an opportunity.
Instead of grieving, I will glorify;
Instead of worrying, I will worship.
That I might rather bear my cross,
To share my Christ, and wear my crown.

— So we do not lose heart. Though our outer self is wasting away, our inner self is being renewed day by day. For this light momentary affliction is preparing us for an eternal weight of glory beyond all comparison, as we look not to the things that are seen but to the things that are unseen. For the things that are seen are transient, but the things that are unseen are eternal. 2 Corinthians 4:16-18

— Do not fear what you are about to suffer. Behold, the devil is about to throw some of you into prison, that you may be tested, and for ten days you will have tribulation. Be faithful unto death, and I will give you the crown of life. Revelation 2:10

"The reason so many of us struggle so intensely with adversity is that we have yet to adopt God's perspective and priorities." — Charles Stanley

Dichotomous Flight

Oh, blessed thought—
Every departing step
On his prodigal path
Prompts an opposite
Flight in me.
The farther he runs from You,
The more I push into You.
As he wrenches away,
I tenaciously cling.
Every newsflash
Of further rebellion
Drives me
With desperation
To Your Word
And Your throne.
When he seeks escape,
I pursue Your embrace.
He retreats into darkness,
I advance toward Your light.
So, even as I pray
For him to turn around—
To recognize Your love,
Always available—
To return to the comforts of home,
I praise You
That his departure
Triggers deeper dependence
Than I have ever known.

— For their feet run to evil. Proverbs 1:16a

— With my whole heart I seek you; let me not wander from your command-ments! // I will run in the way of your commandments when you enlarge my heart! // Your word is a lamp to my feet and a light to my path. Psalm 119:10, 32, 105

The Privilege of Prayer

Abba Father,

Bend Your ear.

I'm on Your lap again.

Calling on You

In my difficult hour,

Appealing to

Your measureless power,

Submitting to

Your supreme authority,

Cherishing this rare

Gift of intimacy,

Honoring Your wisdom,

Your parental role,

Waiting for You, Lord,

To reconcile my soul.

Abba Father,

Please draw near

And hold me tighter then.

— *For you did not receive the spirit of slavery to fall back into fear, but you have received the spirit of adoption as sons, by whom we cry, "Abba! Father!"* Romans 8:15

— *And this is the confidence that we have toward him, that if we ask anything according to his will he hears us. And if we know that he hears us in whatever we ask, we know that we have the requests that we have asked of him.* 1 John 5:14-15

Silent Scream

I have no words;
You groan for me.
Amid silent screams
You intercede.
How do I pray?—
My understanding dim,
Unaware of what I
Need for him,
Unclear, the way
That I should go—
The Holy Spirit
Knows
And brings my tears,
My wordless cries—
Too deep to express—
Before Your eyes.
I crave Your strength
When I am weak.
Your wisdom,
Your way,
I seek.
Stand in the gap,
Bridge the chasm between;
I need not fear the silence
For You will intervene.

— *Likewise the Spirit helps us in our weakness. For we do not know what to pray for as we ought, but the Spirit himself intercedes for us with groanings too deep for words.* Romans 8:26

— *The LORD will fight for you, and you have only to be silent.* Exodus 14:14

Identifying With the Father

Parenthood
Both greatest gift
And toughest trial
Simultaneous
Joy and sorrow
Offspring open
Eyes to eternal truth
Oh, the wondrous
Recognition of
Your presence
At their birth
Then, the worrisome
Recognition of
Your pain
At their rebellion
Ah, the wounding
Recognition of
Your patience
At their persistence
But the warm
Recognition of
Your pleasure
At their return
An open door
To understanding
Your heart,
My heavenly Father

— *My son, do not despise the LORD's discipline or be weary of his reproof, for the LORD reproves him whom he loves, as a father the son in whom he delights.* Proverbs 3:11-12

Still

The enemy encroaches,
Seeking to enslave,
Pursuing relentlessly.
I feel the danger
Nipping at our heels.
Be still!
As burly waves
Threaten to sink my vessel
And carry it to the depths,
I fear my Lord is
Sleeping through this storm.
Be still!
Yet Your Word
Reveals Your purpose
Still.
With a wall of water on the left
And a wall of water on the right,
Horses, chariots, horsemen
Following fast behind,
You remind:
"The Lord will fight for you;
You need only to…
Be still." (Exodus 14:14)
Your people passed through on dry land,
While not one Egyptian survived,
And when they saw how You had saved,
Fear and trust took hold inside.
When the Amorite armies
Came against Joshua, Lord,

You took more by hailstones
Than by sword;
The sun and moon You stilled,
Till they declared,
"Surely the Lord was fighting for Israel." (Joshua 10:14)
When vast armies of Moabites and Ammonites
Came against Jehoshaphat,
He cried out,
"We do not know what to do,
But our eyes are upon You." (2 Chronicles 20:12 NIV)
Your words to them still enthrall,
As You nudge me to recall:
"Do not be afraid or discouraged…
For the battle is not yours, but God's." (2 Chronicles 20:15 NIV)
Your steadfast instruction
When waging war
Is and has always been,
"Do not be fainthearted or afraid; do not panic…
For the LORD your God is the one
Who goes with you
To fight for you." (Deuteronomy 20:3-4 NIV)
"Stand still and see this great thing
That the LORD will do." (1 Samuel 12:16)
He, it is, who fights for you.
Even Your disciples
Feared the storm,
Worried their Lord
Their stress ignored.
If You can rebuke
The wind and waves
To make them

Still,

You can rebuke

My fear and doubt

To make me

Still.

Your promise remains:

"You will keep in perfect peace

Those whose minds are steadfast,

Because they trust in you." (Isaiah 26:3 NIV)

Your purpose persists:

You deliver us

"So that all the kingdoms of the earth

May know that you LORD

Are the only God." (Isaiah 37:20 NIV)

Lord, I beg,

Help silence me

To wait and watch

Your victory,

To make our stories testify

When Satan seeks to terrify

And into peril we are thrust,

Our way, to You, we must entrust.

Then, I will be…

Still

For You are God…

Still.

— *Be still and know that I am God.* Psalm 46:10

Actions and Reactions

I wait
    I wonder
        I worry
I watch
    I warn
        I weep
I wrestle
    I wallow
        I whine

He wants
    He wanders
        He weaves
He wastes
    He weakens
        He wrecks
He wrongs
    He worsens
        He wounds

    But You...
        You witness
            You waive
               You work

        You whisper
            You waken
               You woo
        You welcome
            You wash
               You WIN!

— *You have kept count of my tossings; put my tears in your bottle. Are they not in your book?* Psalm 56:8

— *I have said these things to you, that in me you may have peace. In the world you will have tribulation. But take heart; I have overcome the world.* John 16:33

Standing in the Breach

At times, I'm so vexed I cannot find speech,
Yet, You have called me to stand in the breach.

When the Israelites vexed You
With their rebellion,
Faithlessly forming
Their golden calf,
You would have destroyed them
Had Moses not stood in the breach.
One man,
One cry,
One plea.
Standing between them and Thee.

The breach is that gap
Between Your holiness
And our waywardness.
Sin creates a divide
And Your great love
Cannot but burn white hot.

So as Moses stood, now I stand,
One soul,
One cry,
One plea,
Standing between my child and Thee.

I rely on the chief intercessor
Who, by His sacrifice,
Stood in the gap

Between Your holiness
And our rebellion,
Crossing the chasm
To be the righteousness
We cannot muster.
One Son,
One death,
One salvation,
Standing to provide our reconciliation.

When my prodigal appears out of reach,
I will rejoice, then, to stand in the breach.

— *On your walls, O Jerusalem, I have set watchmen; all the day and all the night they shall never be silent. You who put the LORD in remembrance, take no rest. Isaiah 62:6*

— *And I sought for a man among them who should build up the wall and stand in the breach before me for the land, that I should not destroy it, but I found none. Ezekiel 22:30*

Ready to Rejoice

I'm ready, Lord. Please don't delay.
Can I call my friends and neighbors
To join me in this hoped-for day
After prayer's fervent labors?
This answer so long-awaited,
My persistence now recompensed,
His return celebrated,
Heaven's joy will be immense.
I'll praise You in the morning
When his feet shall cease to roam.
All will see his adorning,
And know he's, at last, come home.

— *And let us not grow weary of doing good, for in due season we will reap, if we do not give up.* Galatians 6:9

— *Rejoice in hope, be patient in tribulation, be constant in prayer.* Romans 12:12

RESENTMENT

— *Now his older son was in the field, and as he came and drew near to the house, he heard music and dancing. And he called one of the servants and asked what these things meant. And he said to him, "Your brother has come, and your father has killed the fattened calf, because he has received him back safe and sound." But he was angry and refused to go in. His father came out and entreated him, but he answered his father, "Look, these many years I have served you, and I never disobeyed your command, yet you never gave me a young goat, that I might celebrate with my friends. But when this son of yours came, who has devoured your property with prostitutes, you killed the fattened calf for him!"* Luke 15:25-30

Rein Him In, Lord

"Well-broke: The horse is well-trained and can be relied on to perform reliably and safely…. The horse will be quiet, obedient, and will not be spooked easily."

"Broke-to-death: means a horse is well-trained, quiet and is a safe ride for almost anyone." — The Spruce Pets — Broke Horse Guide: https://www. thesprucepets.com/what-is-broke-horse-1886596

"Blinders: Horses have peripheral vision, which means they can end up running off course unless they are made to remain focused…. Horses sometimes need to be made to focus and blinders keep the horse's eye focused on what is ahead, rather than what is at the side or behind. That is why race horses are often given blinders—for the purpose of keeping them focused when racing round a racecourse…. If a horse decides to take a different route, it will simply take the jockey with it, so this can pose problems. Troublesome racehorses are fitted with blinders for their own safety and the jockey's safety." — http://www.dallasequestriancenter. com/why-do-horses-wear-blinders/

I'm a "well-broke" horse.
I abide by regulations,
Walking next to my Master,
Following His commands.
If I sense an order,
I seek to obey.
Is that why my colt
Stirs such anger within?
Do I have elder-brother rage
At his lack of compliance?
He kicks against the goads,
Ruinous resistance;
He only hurts himself

When he flouts the Master's lead.
Will experience teach him?
Or will he remain a bucking bronco,
Spirited, uncontrolled?
He "roots," goes his own direction.
He kicks to defend himself,
To rid himself of discomfort.
It takes more energy
To balk than to obey.
Harness him, quiet him, Lord.
Take him down that Damascus road.
Cover his eyes with "blinders,"
And break him, Lord,
Until he's pliable,
"broke-to-death."

— *The sacrifices of God are a broken spirit; a broken and contrite heart, O God, you will not despise.* Psalm 51:17

Praying Onlookers

How can I regret asking others
To petition Your throne, Lord?
Yet prayer support laced with judgment
Feels neither welcome nor helpful.
"Is your child still allowed to continue… ?"

      Yes, I have a choice in the matter
      Yet I choose to encourage
      My child to pursue that which
      I know might kill them!
      Thanks for alerting me to the solution—
      Executing and enforcing
      Proper rules will surely eliminate
      This errant behavior.

Or the prayer expressing my child
No longer belongs to You
Because he is pursuing the wrong path.

      Even David,
      A man after God's own heart,
      Wandered from the way
      While held in the Father's hand.
      It's easier to judge
      Another's wanderings
      Than to recognize one's own.

Yet, once again, You beckon Lord—"Forgive!
Forgive them, for they know not what they do!
Forgive them, for they may not see their rebellion!
Forgive them, for they mean well, but express poorly!
Forgive, for I have forgiven you these exact faults, my child!"
So, thank You for Your forgiveness, Lord,

When I'm oblivious to how my words condescend and offend,

When I foolishly believe my prodigal's return depends on me,

When I try to solve problems in my strength and understanding,

When I point to the missteps of others, ignoring my stumbling feet.

Thank You for revealing hidden waywardness I hadn't recognized.

— Be kind to one another, tenderhearted, forgiving one another, as God in Christ forgave you. Ephesians 4:32

"To live above with saints we love will certainly be glory. To live below with saints we know, well, that's another story." — Author unknown

Pardon Me, Lord, My Pride is Showing

I took the scalpel out today
To pull back the outer layer,
To investigate down to the heart.
I don't want this road, Lord!
But why don't I want it?
Yes, I want to shield my child from disaster;
But looking deeper, I see,
I don't want it for me either.
Being the parent who failed to raise
The God-fearing, law-abiding child,
Looks bad on me.
Others will judge me
On my child's choices.
Is that what wounds me so?
What others think?
So that's the heart of the matter—
My own swollen pride!
But, here's the real problem—
I cannot excavate my error.
You are the master surgeon!
Only You can rid me of my prideful offense
At my position.
Cut out that root of all sin—pride!
I do not deserve better than I'm given.
I am not master of my universe.
But, You are!
I humble myself in Your sight.
Root out my heart of stone;
Replace it with a heart of flesh.

Help me to rely on You

And stand before God, not man.

No, kneel before God, disregarding man!

— *Whatever you do, work heartily, as for the Lord and not for men.*
Colossians 3:23

— *And I will give you a new heart, and a new spirit I will put within you.*
And I will remove the heart of stone from your flesh and give you a heart of
flesh. Ezekiel 36:26

Bring Me to My Senses

I hear the pointing fingers,
Though seldom words are said;
Are those my own voices
Swirling within my head?
I see the subtle lifted nose—
"I would have done it right."
My self-incrimination grows
As I tread through this night.
I smell the hesitation,
Afraid this blight might spread;
If I had known the path
We'd walk, I too would dread.
I taste the bitterness
Of friendship pulled away
Because I ignore their advice
Nor walk their way.
I touch a tender nerve,
A proof of sin's demise,
Satan's sick infringement
And insidious lies.
You bring me to my senses
In spite of all my pain;
It matters not what others think
But only what I'll gain
When I look to You for answers,
When I listen for Your voice,
When I allow Your wisdom
To touch my internal noise.
I try to make sense of this,

My guilt, their looks, Your view;

I lay my feelings at Your feet,

I give them all to You.

— It is dangerous to be concerned with what others think of you, but if you trust the LORD, you are safe. Proverbs 29:25 (GNB)

Unconditional Grace

They were "friends," Lord,

Supposedly siblings in the faith.

Missionaries

Seeking to save the lost.

But my lost son,

My ineffective parenting

Didn't qualify.

They declared love for You

And for those drowning in darkness

Yet would not extend love to

Your own who failed or wandered.

Instead, they severed relationship,

Withdrew in superiority.

Father, make me more like You,

Always extending grace,

No matter if it's withheld,

Forgiving those who fall short,

Because, far too often,

Like the resentful brother,

My love is conditional, too.

— *If anyone says, "I love God," and hates his brother, he is a liar; for he who does not love his brother whom he has seen cannot love God whom he has not seen.* 1 John 4:20

Prodigal Catch-22

"Catch-22: A problematic situation for which the only solution is
denied by a circumstance inherent in the problem or by a rule"
— *Merriam-Webster*

He needs new friends—
Better friends—
Friends with a
Positive influence.
How can I blame
His old friends for fleeing
In the face of his new fixation?
I would urge
My own child
To run from such a one.
Bad company
Corrupts good character.
They suck you into
The quicksand
As you attempt to rescue them
From the oozing muck.
So I watch him sink,
Clasping hands
With fellow muck swimmers.
What a vexing problem—
Good company doesn't
Correct bad character;
Good company recognizes danger
And runs as fast as legs can carry,
As it well should.
The sinking wayward

Need You far more

Than better friends.

Only You can lift them from the mire

So that is my prayer, my heart's desire.

— *Do not be misled: "Bad company corrupts good character."* 1 Corinthians 15:33 (NIV)

— *Save me, O God! For the waters have come up to my neck. I sink in deep mire, where there is no foothold; I have come into deep waters, and the flood sweeps over me. // Deliver me from sinking in the mire; let me be delivered from my enemies and from the deep waters. Let not the flood sweep over me, or the deep swallow me up, or the pit close its mouth over me.* Psalm 69:1-2, 14-15

Deeply Disgraced

Oh, depth of disgrace,

Embarrassing space.

How I hoped he'd stay in line

So I could proudly say he's mine;

Instead, I cringe and shudder within

At each ignominious dip into sin.

Then I remember my own inclination,

My sullying marks on Your salvation.

Do others see me and say I've disgraced

You, Lord, by my insistent embrace

Of things that are dirty, that leave me unclean,

That tarnish Your reputation, to those who, sight unseen,

Deny Your power because my example demeans

The evidence of transformation I wish to proclaim?

Forgive me, Lord, and help me forgive him

For each and every betrayal, each stifling sin

That detracts from Your glory,

Besmirches Your story.

I don't want to disgrace You,

Nor fall from Your grace, too.

Help me!

Help him!

Forgive us our sin!

— You who boast in the law dishonor God by breaking the law. For, as it is written, "The name of God is blasphemed among the Gentiles because of you." Romans 2:23-24

— O God, you know my folly; the wrongs I have done are not hidden from you. Let not those who hope in you be put to shame through me, O Lord

GOD of hosts; let not those who seek you be brought to dishonor through me, O God of Israel. Psalm 69:5-6

"You are the only Bible some unbelievers will ever read, and your life is under scrutiny every day. What do others learn from you? Do they see an accurate picture of your God?" — John MacArthur

Sibling in the Shadow

He's a compliant son
By innate inclination,
But equally fearing
Guilt by association;
If he steps out of line
They'll think he's like his brother.
He sees the pain and anguish;
Won't create more for his mother.
And why should he be put
In a secondary sphere?
All energy and focus
On one who won't adhere
To the rules he gladly follows,
To the line he easily walks,
Always in the shadow
Of wherever that one stalks.
He didn't make this problem
Yet he's asked to sacrifice
All normalcy in life—
A cruel and unjust price.
I pour out my fears, Lord:
Will he curry favor
Relying on the merits
Of virtuous behavior?
Or will he be confused?—
Love isn't based on action,
Yet it seems intensified
By every new infraction.
Will he feel forgotten,
Like an overlooked one
When every crisis moves us

To reach that other son?
Will he resent the pain
His brother often causes?
I see how he suffers.
I recognize his losses.
Lord, help me parent this one
With equal grace and love,
Following the example
Of my Father up above.
I don't want to pray less when
He seems to need less prayer,
Nor fail to show great love
Because he's always there.
Lord, help me to show him
His compliance is a gift,
But we're not depending on him
To give our hearts a lift
When the other pulls us down.
We love them separately,
No matter their actions,
We love them desperately.
Don't let our desperation
For the one rule out the other,
Lord, bless him as he stands
In the shadow of his brother.

— *For by grace you have been saved through faith. And this is not your own doing; it is the gift of God, not a result of works, so that no one may boast.* Ephesians 2:8-9

— *But if it is by grace, it is no longer on the basis of works; otherwise grace would no longer be grace.* Romans 11:6

REINFORCED REJOICING

— And he said to him, "Son, you are always with me, and all that is mine is yours. It was fitting to celebrate and be glad, for this your brother was dead, and is alive; he was lost, and is found. Luke 15:31-32

Lord, I Want the Pen

I don't want this story.

Conflict, tension,

Heart-wrenching fear,

Nail-biting uncertainty.

I want a tamer tale.

Safety, security,

Lung-filling calm,

Eye-closing tranquility.

I've tried countless times

To wrench the pen from Your grasp.

My will. My way.

My plot. My purpose.

I want a light-hearted comedy,

Not a heavy-handed tragedy.

Yet You write on,

Crafting a far better biography.

Redemption sagas

Aren't set on Easy Street.

No dirt means no need to wash.

And that is the heart of Your narrative:

Vast violation requires great grace;

The deeper the debt, the fuller the forgiveness.

You redeem what is broken;

You reconcile what is far.

And the songs of praise are sweeter

Because heaven has more joy

For one repenting sinner

Than ninety-nine softer stories.

Redeem me and mine

From the hand of the foe
To shout Your salvation.

— *Shall a faultfinder contend with the Almighty? He who argues with God, let him answer it.* Job 40:2

Home

Your love is
Rich,
Strong,
Sustaining.
My way was
Wrong,
Self-centered,
Complaining.
I wanted more
Than You had given;
I was
Ungrateful,
Selfish,
Driven.
The alternative
I sought
Came up dry;
It couldn't
Possibly satisfy,
While all the while
You offered home,
Always available
Should I cease to roam.
I cannot continue
My own way;
I must return
Without delay.
Why would I
Ever choose the cold

Over the warmth

Of Your protected fold?

— I will give them a heart to know that I am the LORD, and they shall be my people and I will be their God, for they shall return to me with their whole heart. Jeremiah 24:7

Open My Eyes

My sight is limited, Lord.
I only see the enemy,
Vast,
Troublesome,
Menacing,
His clouds hang
Ominous
Over me,
Legions of demons
Desperate to snatch my son,
A billowing storm
I cannot outrun.
My sight is one-dimensional
In a three-dimensional realm.
How often I forget
That You are at the helm.
I fail to see the horses,
The chariots of fire,
Fighting when my
Circumstances seem
Most dire.
You have not surrendered;
Your victory is sure.
When my eyes view
Your spiritual plane,
I know I can endure
Whatever Satan
Throws at me.
So, whenever things look grim,

Remind me there are more with us

Than those who are with him.

— *Little children, you are from God and have overcome them, for he who is in you is greater than he who is in the world.* 1 John 4:4

— *And these are but the outer fringe of his works; how faint the whisper we hear of him! Who then can understand the thunder of his power?* Job 26:14 (NIV)

"While it looks like things are out of control, behind the scenes there is a God who has not surrendered authority." — A. W. Tozer

Proving Ground

During this dark night,

On this sacred ground,

You try me.

As we wrestle

May it reveal

What I'm made of,

May my allegiance ring true,

My dependence sound strong,

My devotion cling fast.

As we wrestle,

Though the fight is fierce,

I will see

Your faithfulness,

Your constancy,

Your dependability,

Despite trials and obstacles.

As You prove trustworthy,

Help me to trust;

As You prove steadfast,

Help me stand firm.

At daybreak

Though I limp

I will clutch Your blessing.

— *For you, O God, have tested us; you have tried us as silver is tried. You brought us into the net; you laid a crushing burden on our backs; you let men ride over our heads; we went through fire and through water; yet you have brought us out to a place of abundance.* Psalm 66:10-12

— *For I bear on my body the scars that show I belong to Jesus.* Galatians 6:17b (NLT)

Not by Chance

In guilt, I think we cast his lot,
Hereditary forces compelling—
His father's brother
Addicted to drinking,
His mother's cousin
Unhinged from smoking
The same substance he craves.
Our temperance counts for nothing.

But Scripture
Tells a different story.
This personal
Background inventory
Was part of Your
Knowledge a priori;
You will use it
For Your glory.

—*The lot is cast into the lap, but its every decision is from the LORD.*
Proverbs 16:33

— *Consider the work of God; who can make straight what he has made crooked? In the day of prosperity be joyful, and in the day of adversity consider: God has made the one as well as the other, so that man may not find out anything that will be after him.* Ecclesiastes 7:13-14

Prodigal Testimony

I stood on the path
Staring.
His steps had
Veered
Into the wilderness
Tearing.
His footprints
Disappeared.
I couldn't get my
Bearing.
He'd chosen the way
Uncleared.
I was deeply
Despairing;
This child that I
Reared
Was fumbling,
Erring,
Just as I
Feared.
But, Lord, You were
Declaring
His name could be
Cleared,
His sins, though
Glaring,
Washed and heart
Cheered,
For You were

Preparing

To welcome as he

Neared,

Your grace

Unsparing,

Your love

Persevered

Despite Satan's

Ensnaring.

You—above all—are

Revered

In this story we're

Sharing.

— *But where sin increased, grace abounded all the more.* Romans 5:20b

— *But I do not count my life of any value nor as precious to myself, if only I may finish my course and the ministry that I received from the Lord Jesus, to testify to the gospel of the grace of God.* Acts 20:24

May Our Prodigal Story Make Us Run to You

Lord, his wandering
Has brought me to the end of myself.
I recognize my efforts
To handle this on my own.
How do others
Endure this without You?
I pray our experiences with a prodigal
Will open our eyes to our own prodigal nature
And propel us back into Your arms,
Recognizing anew our desperate need of You.
We are dead,
Satisfied with cornhusks
When we could be dining on steak.
Save us, Lord.
Give us Your life.
Redeem us from wandering
Within the enemy's field.
Return us to Your loving arms,
Saved, sanctified, healed.

— For we do not want you to be unaware, brothers, of the affliction we experienced in Asia. For we were so utterly burdened beyond our strength that we despaired of life itself. Indeed, we felt that we had received the sentence of death. But that was to make us rely not on ourselves but on God who raises the dead. 2 Corinthians 1:8-9

Surrendered

I give back this life,
Given to me
With wisdom and purpose
I cannot see.
When my life feels useless
Help me to know
You're guiding and leading,
Making me grow.

I give back this trial;
Use as You will.
I'm yielded and waiting,
Humble and still.
When placed in Your power
It yields two-fold;
Though dross when in my hands,
In Yours, it's gold.

I give back this child
You gave to me.
Please guide him and save him,
Shape patiently,
Until he is Yours, Lord,
Putty in hand,
Molded in Your image,
'Mid trials He'll stand.

Everything that I have
Has come from You.
Any bit of value

You must imbue.

I cannot hold it back,

Must surrender,

Every minute detail

For Your splendor.

— And now we thank you, our God, and praise your glorious name. But who am I, and what is my people, that we should be able thus to offer willingly? For all things come from you, and of your own have we given you. 1 Chronicles 29:13-14

The Gift of Prodigal Parenting

Lord,

Thank You

For the gift

My prodigal son provides.

His detour presents a privilege.

His direction dispenses an excellent education.

His departure drives me closer to You.

Every experience along the way reveals Your truth.

I am overwhelmed by the outstanding opportunity to observe

The patient, persistent power of the Holy Spirit,

The comprehensive compassion of the Heavenly Father,

The significant sacrifice of the Son,

Attributes I might not perceive

Apart from this path

Persistently pursued by

My prodigal

Child.

— *What if God, desiring to show his wrath and to make known his power, has endured with much patience vessels of wrath prepared for destruction.* Romans 9:22

— *He saved us, not because of works done by us in righteousness, but according to his own mercy, by the washing of regeneration and renewal of the Holy Spirit, whom he poured out on us richly through Jesus Christ our Savior.* Titus 3:5-6

Conveying Comfort

Take my words
And make them water
To soothe another sin-scorched soul.

Use this trial
That I am treading
To wrap a wound and make it whole.

Open my eyes,
My understanding,
To perceive another's pain.

Grant me grace,
That ripples round me,
To soften hurts that they sustain.

— *Blessed be the God and Father of our Lord Jesus Christ, the Father of mercies and God of all comfort, who comforts us in all our affliction, so that we may be able to comfort those who are in any affliction, with the comfort with which we ourselves are comforted by God. For as we share abundantly in Christ's sufferings, so through Christ we share abundantly in comfort too. If we are afflicted, it is for your comfort and salvation; and if we are comforted, it is for your comfort, which you experience when you patiently endure the same sufferings that we suffer.* 2 Corinthians 1:3-6

"I love when people that have been through hell walk out of the flames carrying buckets of water for those still consumed by the fire." — Stephanie Sparkles (Google images: concern quotes)

SUPPLEMENTAL SCRIPTURES
& JOURNALING QUESTIONS

Prayer for a Wayward Teen

Luke 16:15; Proverbs 30:12; Proverbs 12:15

1) What God-given boundaries have you resisted?

2) How might they have been positioned to protect you?

Residual Stench

Proverbs 11:27; Romans 12:2a

1) What residual consequences cling to your child or family?

2) How might you give those consequences back to God to use as He wills?

Wounds in the Enemy's Field

Proverbs 14:12; 2 Corinthians 11:3; James 4:7; Romans 16:20a;
1 Peter 5:8-10; 2 Thessalonians 2:8

1) What reverberations, ramifications, upheaval, or conflict has spilled from your prodigal onto the lives of those around him/her?

2) How might you specifically pray for God's protection from the wounds inflicted while in the enemy's field?

Who's the Prodigal?

Romans 2:8; 2 Timothy 3:2; 1 Corinthians 13:5; Hebrews 3:13

1) Where do you find it difficult to submit or see God's refining as a blessing?

2) How might recognizing your own prodigal tendencies help you understand and forgive your child's prodigal behavior?

Runaway Train

Jeremiah 17:7-8; Isaiah 43:2; Psalm 23:4; Psalm 56:3; Matthew 6:34; Psalm 39:7; John 14:27; 1 Peter 5:6-7; Isaiah 35:4; Proverbs 3:5-6.

1) In what way is your child accelerating toward certain destruction?

2) When have you felt God's supernatural peace in the midst of uncertainty and chaos?

3) How has prayer calmed anxious thoughts in the past?

Lying With the Dogs

1 Corinthians 15:33 (GNB); Galatians 6:7; Proverbs 4:14-19; Proverbs 5:22; Numbers 32:23b; Proverbs 13:20; Proverbs 14:7; Proverbs 16:29 (ISV); Proverbs 22:3, 5, 24-25; Psalm 1:1

1) What role have friends played in your child's rebellion?

2) How might you pray for God to allow disillusionment with negative influences to provide wisdom for future friend choices?

Clouded Perspective

Ephesians 4:17-19; James 1:14-15; 1 Corinthians 2:14 (NIV); Romans 1:18, 21-22; Hebrews 3:12-14; Titus 1:15b; 1 Timothy 4:2; Philippians 3:19; John 9:39a; Matthew 6:22-23; Matthew 13:15

1) In what way is your child's vision blurred?

2) In what specific ways do you want God to clear their vision?

Double-minded

James 1:5-8; James 4:8; 1 John 5:14-15; Hebrews 11:1, 6

1) When have you experienced wavering faith?

2) How does fixing your eyes on God and trusting His provision every moment help fight the waves of fear and doubt?

Baggage Complicates

Luke 11:17; Colossians 3:12-15; Psalm 133:1; 1 Corinthians 14:33a; Ephesians 4:3 (NLT); Romans 8:26a; Isaiah 30:18

1) If you co-parent, when have you experienced division concerning the best approach to your child's rebellion?

2) How might your own weaknesses and vulnerabilities be influencing your responses?

3) How do God's promises free you from the fear that you may fail to respond to your child's rebellion appropriately?

4) How have you seen God balance grace and truth in His response to your own prodigal nature?

Frequent Flyer on If Only Airlines

Hosea 6:1; 2 Peter 2:9; Philippians 3:13; Romans 8:28;
Isaiah 43:18-19; Philippians 3:13-14; Psalm 139:16; 1 Peter 5:10;
Proverbs 16:33; Philippians 4:19; Jeremiah 29:11; 1 Peter 4:12-13

1) Have you flown on If Only Airlines?

2) Make your own list, turning each if only into an only if.

When Ignorance Ignites Imagination

Psalm 33:18; 1 Peter 1:13; Ephesians 1:18; Psalm 3:5-6; Luke 1:37;
Hebrews 10:23; Philippians 1:6; Psalm 130:5; Isaiah 43:2;
2 Corinthians 4:17-18; 1 John 4:18

1) When has the unknown driven your imagination into dangerous territory?

2) How might His presence temper the thoughts in your mind?

3) When you don't know where they are, what verses remind you that He is with them?

The Divine Alchemist

2 Corinthians 1:8-9; Psalm 68:19; Psalm 55:22; Romans 8:18, 28; Psalm 23:4; Proverbs 17:3; Job 23:10; Jeremiah 17:5-8; James 1:12; Hebrews 12:11

1) How has God turned burdens to blessings for you in the past?

2) How might the thorns and thistles of your journey prod an unexpected song?

Chisel Me

Isaiah 64:8; Ephesians 2:10; Philippians 1:6; Job 13:23; Jeremiah 18:3-8; Romans 9:17-24

1) How has your child exposed your own vulnerabilities and inadequacies?

2) How is God shaping you through the process of parenting your child?

When Comparison Steals My Joy

Proverbs 14:30; 1 Corinthians 3:3; Exodus 20:17; Galatians 5:26; 1 Peter 2:1; 2 Corinthians 10:12; 1 Corinthians 13:12; 1 Corinthians 2:16a

1) When have you allowed comparison to steal your joy?

2) When have you struggled with the misperception that you some-how earned your child's rebellion while other parents earned their child's good fortune?

3) How might the thorns be keeping you from seeing the beauty of the flower?

Distracted by Other Runners

Hebrews 12:1; 1 Corinthians 9:26-27; 2 Timothy 4:7-8; Philippians 3:14; Philippians 4:13; Galatians 5:7; Matthew 24:13; James 1:12; Isaiah 40:29, 31; 2 Corinthians 12:10

1) Who distracts you from your race and why?

2) How might you pray for God to excise your envy?

3) In what way is it better to limp while dependent on God than to breeze through life independent of Him?

Clenched Hands

Psalm 88:4-6, 14; Isaiah 45:7; John 14:1; John 13:7; Genesis 50:20; 2 Corinthians 4:17-18; Psalm 27:13-14; Jude 1:22; Hebrews 3:12; Hebrews 11:1; Matthew 8:26

1) Do you struggle with feeling your situation is an oversight on God's part?

2) Where have you presumed to know best?

3) How might you pray for God's forgiveness for your unbelief and remind yourself that you will not be His first mistake?

While on the Wheel

Ephesians 2:10 (NLT); Isaiah 29:16; Isaiah 45:9; James 1:2-4; Romans 9:21; Romans 12:2; Psalm 119:50, 73

1) How have God's pressures and restraints made you more fit as a vessel for His use?

2) What careless complaints have you uttered while on the wheel?

Only You Fit

Ecclesiastes 3:11; Jeremiah 17:9; Ecclesiastes 9:3b; Romans 1:18-22; Ephesians 3:19 (NLT); John 7:38; 1 John 2:16

1) What is your child attempting to fill his/her spiritual hole with for now?

2) Have you ever sought to fill your hole with insufficient substitutes?

Yearning for Yesterday

Genesis 3:24; Isaiah 43:18-19; Philippians 3:13-14; 2 Corinthians 5:2-4, 17-19

1) In what ways do you yearn for yesterday?

2) How can you acknowledge the nostalgia yet "press on toward the goal for the prize of the upward call of God?"

Send Him a Nathan

Proverbs 21:2; Proverbs 27:6a; Proverbs 13:12; John 8:44b

1) What frustrations have you experienced when your advice goes unheeded?

2) How might you pray for God to send someone else to confront or persuade your child?

Shatter Satan's Strongholds

Hebrews 12:1; 1 Peter 5:8; 2 Corinthians 2:11; Ephesians 2:8; Acts 4:12; Titus 3:5; Lamentations 3:26; 1 Peter 1:18-19; 1 Timothy 2:5; Psalm 71:15

1) What Satanic strongholds suffocate your child's life?

2) How does watching this process make you feel helpless?

3) In what way could your situation be used to show others how God can save?

When I Fear the Water

Isaiah 30:20; Isaiah 43:2a; 2 Samuel 22:17; Jeremiah 17:7-8; Matthew 11:28-30; Jonah 2:5; Lamentations 3:54; Psalm 18:16 (NIV); Psalm 69:1-2, 14-15; Psalm 124:4-5; Psalm 144:7

1) How does total trust keep you from sinking?

2) How has God been with you in your deep waters?

3) Could you share those moments with your child?

Revive My Heart

2 Corinthians 12:9; 2 Chronicles 20:15b-17; 1 Samuel 17:47; James 4:7; Deuteronomy 20:1-4; Deuteronomy 31:6; Exodus 14:14

1) In what ways do you feel beaten, helpless, or drained?

2) When fear of losing this battle saps all of your strength, what promises do you lean on?

3) How does trusting His ability to conquer death and sin help when your knees are weak?

Dancing With the Worst-case Scenario

Isaiah 35:4; John 14:1, 27; Joshua 1:9; Psalm 34:4; Psalm 56:3; Psalm 94:19; Romans 8:38-39; Proverbs 3:5-6; Jeremiah 17:7-8; 1 Peter 5:7

1) What worst-case scenario pulls you into a dance of fear?

2) When have reminders of God's sovereignty helped you drown out those tales of woe?

I Know Your Extravagant Grace

Isaiah 59:1-3; Acts 17:30; 2 Timothy 4:4; 2 Timothy 3:2; Ezekiel 14:7; Ephesians 2:12

1) In what ways do you identify with your prodigal child?

2) How has God extended extravagant grace to you?

3) How can praising Him for wooing you back reinforce hope for your child's future?

Remind Me of the Morning

Jeremiah 31:16-17; Acts 26:18; Colossians 1:13; Isaiah 42:16; Luke 1:78-79; Job 11:17-19

1) When have you been plagued by the 3:00-a.m. mind?

2) When things look bleak, what helps you remember the inevitability of morning?

3) What joys do you think await you when your darkness lifts and morning comes?

4) If the end isn't what you'd imagined or the night seems long, how will you cling to God?

Revive

Deuteronomy 30:19; James 1:14; Exodus 2:23; Psalm 34:6; Genesis 2:7

1) In what way is your child choosing a life of death?

2) Identify the needs that drive your child's rebellion.

3) What might his/her future testimony look like?

Carving a Path to Peace Through Praise

Psalm 4:8; Isaiah 26:3; John 16:33; Ephesians 2:14; Romans 8:6; 2 Corinthians 13:11

1) How has praising God helped you prune back the weeds of distress in the past?

2) How can you nurture an attitude of gratitude in the midst of great agony?

3) Specifically, how has worship enlarged your view of God while diminishing your view of circumstances?

Progression to Enemy Flight

1 Peter 5:8-9; Ephesians 6:11-17; 1 John 5:4-5; John 10:10;
James 4:7; Romans 8:37; Joshua 23:10; Hebrews 4:12

1) When has it felt like you were fighting your child rather than
the spiritual forces of darkness?

2) What weapons does God equip you with to trigger
the enemy's flight?

3) Identify who and how you need to attack.

Fortify My Response

Hebrews 4:16; Romans 8:35-39 (NLT); Philippians 4:13; Isaiah
30:15b; Joshua 23:10; 2 Timothy 1:7; 2 Corinthians 1:8-11; 2
Chronicles 20:12, 15b, 17; Isaiah 50:10; Psalm 91:5-12; James 1:12

1) When have you wanted to go AWOL in this battle for your
child's soul?

2) How can you express candidly what you are up against while still
communicating courage and fearlessness?

3) What helps you persevere in prayer for your child?

Tenuous Calm

Luke 1:37; Romans 8:24-25; Romans 15:4, 13; Psalm 3:2-6 (NIV); Psalm 34:4-7; Psalm 40:1-3; Psalm 94:18-19; Deuteronomy 31:8; Philippians 1:6; 2 Corinthians 4:17-18; Job 6:8

1) When have you experienced moments of tenuous calm?

2) What are your biggest fears when your child is in recovery?

3) When has waiting for your child's return been the most difficult?

Protected by Your Pinions

Psalm 36:7; Psalm 63:7; Isaiah 40:31 (YLT); Deuteronomy 32:11

1) How do you feel covered, sheltered, and shielded under God's protective wings?

2) When storms of destruction rage around you, how can you remind yourself to seek His refuge?

You Steer; I'm Just a Pinion

Proverbs 3:5-6; Isaiah 48:17; Psalm 119:105; Isaiah 58:11; Philippians 4:13; Proverbs 4:25-27; Isaiah 30:21; Mark 9:29; Nehemiah 1:4; 2 Chronicles 20:3; Luke 18:1; James 5:16

1) What would it look like to mesh with God's plans, patterns, and purpose?

2) When have you felt a sense of fulfillment from the opportunity to struggle on behalf of your prodigal?

When Satan Seeks to Pinion

2 Timothy 2:26; John 8:34-36; Acts 8:23; Isaiah 14:3 (KJV); Psalm 116:16; Isaiah 58:6; Psalm 107:13-16

1) When have you felt bound by Satan?

2) Which Satanic shackle in your child's life is hardest to bear?

3) How does dependence on God bring freedom while independence from God brings bondage?

Hide and Seek

Jeremiah 29:13-14; Psalm 63:1 (NIV); Psalm 34:4, 10; Isaiah 55:6; Amos 5:4; Isaiah 65:1-2; Luke 19:10; Psalm 139:1-2; Proverbs 2:4-5; Acts 17:27 (NIV); Psalm 27:4-5; Psalm 32:7 (NIV)

1) When has God felt most hidden?

2) Do you feel you seek Him persistently, or do you sometimes hide from His view?

3) Does your seeking help you to see Him more clearly, and do you feel more clearly seen by Him?

Altered Vision

John 16:20-22; Romans 5:3-4; Colossians 3:2; Jeremiah 29:11; Isaiah 55:8-9; 2 Timothy 4:8; James 1:12; Isaiah 62:3

1) When have you focused too intently on the affliction, grief, or worry?

2) How could you adopt God's perspectives and priorities toward your prodigal's journey?

3) How has your cross led to a crown?

Dichotomous Flight

Philippians 2:16; Isaiah 40:29; Hebrews 12:11-13; 2 Corinthians 4:17; Deuteronomy 13:4; Psalm 63:8; James 4:8; Colossians 3:2; Isaiah 26:9

1) In what way has your prodigal's path led you to deeper dependence on God?

2) In what way has God's Word been a lamp and light leading in the right direction?

The Privilege of Prayer

1 John 3:1a; Galatians 4:6; Philippians 4:6; Luke 11:9; Psalm 34:17; James 5:13a; Psalm 145:18-19; Psalm 141:2; James 1:5; 1 Peter 5:6-7; Isaiah 65:24

1) Jesus sweat drops of blood in prayer prior to His crucifixion. In what way can you identify with His distress when you need to submit to God's authority and wait on God's plan?

2) How has prayer been a privilege in your life?

Silent Scream

Hebrews 7:25; Romans 8:34 (entire chapter really); Exodus 2:23b; 2 Chronicles 14:11 (NLT); Psalm 34:6 (NLT); Psalm 61:2; Psalm 56:8-9; Isaiah 40:29; 2 Corinthians 12:9-10; Philippians 4:13; Psalm 142:3

1) When have you been unable to articulate the agony of your journey?

2) When you scream silently, what are you trying to say to God?

3) When you don't know how best to pray for your child, how can you rely on the Holy Spirit's groans on your behalf?

Identifying With the Father

Genesis 2:7; Psalm 127:3; Hebrews 12:7-11; Psalm 100:3; Psalm 103:13; Proverbs 10:1; Isaiah 64:8; Deuteronomy 32:6

1) In what ways has parenthood been both a gift and a trial?

2) How does this prodigal path help you identify with your heavenly Father?

Still

Psalm 37:7a; Psalm 62:5-6; Psalm 89:9; Isaiah 30:15; Isaiah 41:10-13; Lamentations 3:24-26; Mark 4:39; James 5:7-8

1) When have you felt danger boxing you in and nipping at your heels?

2) When you fear that God is sleeping while your storm rages, what Bible passage calms your fears?

3) What tangible action can you take to be still in the face of this vast enemy?

Actions and Reactions

Psalm 37:7a, 8b; Proverbs 10:1b; Proverbs 12:25 (NLT); Proverbs 19:26; Isaiah 64:4; Matthew 6:27, 34; Philippians 4:19; Hebrews 3:7; 1 Kings 19:11-12; Isaiah 53:5

1) What in this journey causes you to weep the most?

2) How has your prodigal child wounded you?

3) How can knowing God is the final victor help you face those tears and wounds?

Standing in the Breach

Psalm 77:4 (KJV); Psalm 106:23; Philippians 1:19; Ephesians 6:18; James 5:15-16, 19-20; Exodus 32:31-32; Isaiah 53:12b (NLT); 2 Corinthians 1:11; 1 Timothy 2:1-6

1) How has it been a privilege to stand in the breach for your child before God?

2) When you feel insignificant in the face of the trial, how can the intercession of Moses and Christ remind you of the power of your prayer?

Ready to Rejoice

2 Peter 3:9; Psalm 13:1; Psalm 40:17; James 5:7; Colossians 4:2; Luke 18:1; 1 Thessalonians 5:17; Philippians 1:6; Ephesians 6:18; Isaiah 61:10; Luke 15:10

1) Who will you call first when your child turns from rebellion?

2) What helps you persist in prayer's fervent labors?

3) Let your imagination run wild. What will heaven's celebration look like?

Rein Him In, Lord

Romans 8:7, 13; James 4:7; Romans 13:5; Luke 9:23; Galatians 5:24; John 12:24; Romans 6:11-14; Colossians 3:5; Titus 2:12; 1 Timothy 4:7b; Jeremiah 31:18 (KJV)

1) If you are a compliant individual, how do you struggle with elder-brother rage at your prodigal's non-compliance?

2) What self-inflicted harm is your child reaping from flouting the Master's lead?

3) How have you noticed in your own life that it takes more energy to balk than to obey?

4) Are you "broke-to-death" when it comes to your relationship with God?

Praying Onlookers

Matthew 7:1-5; Luke 23:34; Matthew 6:14

1) When have you felt misunderstood or judged by those offering prayer?

2) Have you tried, through rules and regulations, to produce the necessary heart change within your prodigal that only God can produce?

3) Who do you need to forgive for a less-than-helpful response?

4) When have you pointed to the missteps of others while ignoring your own stumbling feet?

Pardon Me, Lord, My Pride is Showing

Luke 5:31; 1 Timothy 3:6 (GNB); Romans 12:3b (NIV); Ezekiel 11:19; Romans 8:31b; Galatians 1:10; 1 Thessalonians 2:4b; John 12:43 (KJV)

1) How have you struggled with wounded pride when your child's behavior reflects badly on you?

2) Are you deluded into thinking you deserve better than you've been given?

3) How can you kneel before the Lord and beg for a heart of flesh?

Bring Me to My Senses

Psalm 34:5, 8; Romans 14:10; 1 John 2:28; Proverbs 2:1-6; Psalm 119:18; John 10:27; 1 Peter 5:7; Galatians 1:10

1) When have your own internal thoughts stirred opinions of judgment that might not have been there?

2) How do you handle the difficult position of bearing the proof of sin's demise?

3) How does disregarding the opinions of man and focusing on your position before God bring you a sense of peace?

4) What feelings do you need to give to God today?

Unconditional Grace

Proverbs 17:17; John 13:34-35; Proverbs 20:6; Colossians 3:13; Mark 11:25; Ephesians 4:32; Luke 6:37; 1 Peter 4:8; Psalm 86:15; James 4:6

1) Have you experienced a severed relationship because of the prodigal path of your child?

2) Are you ever, like the resentful brother, conditional in your love toward others?

3) How can you be more intentional in extending unconditional grace?

Prodigal Catch-22

Proverbs 1:10; Proverbs 4:14-19; Proverbs 12:26; Proverbs 22:24-25; Proverbs 13:20; Psalm 1:1; Psalm 26:4-5; Proverbs 16:29; 1 Corinthians 5:11

1) How do you see your child clasping hands with fellow muck swimmers?

2) When praying for a positive influence from friends feels futile, how can you shift your prayer for God to lift your child from the sinking mire?

Deeply Disgraced

1 John 2:28; Proverbs 19:26; Hebrews 8:12; Ephesians 5:11-12; Psalm 44:15; 1 Peter 1:14; 1 Peter 2:11-12; Philippians 1:27a; Acts 24:16; Ephesians 4:22; 1 Thessalonians 5:22

1) How might you have disgraced God by your inclinations or your embrace of things that tarnish your reputation as a child of God?

2) Are you giving an accurate presentation of the transformation God makes in the lives of His children?

3) How does identifying your own propensity to disgrace your Father help you relate to your child and their struggles?

Sibling in the Shadow

2 Timothy 2:15; Ephesians 2:8-9; Psalm 119:115; James 1:25; Galatians 2:16; Galatians 3:10-11; Romans 9:16; Titus 3:4-5

1) If your prodigal has a sibling, how has that child been overshadowed or forgotten?

2) What sacrifices of normalcy do others in the family face as a result of your prodigal's path?

3) How can you be more intentional in your love and prayers for the compliant child?

Lord, I Want the Pen

Job 42:2; Luke 7:41-43; Luke 15:7; Psalm 107:2

1) If you were writing your own life story, how would it be different?

2) How have you argued with God or found fault with His plans for your life?

3) Why do we prefer Easy Street when other roads lead to richer stories of redemption?

Home

John 14:1-4; 2 Chronicles 7:14; Jeremiah 3:12b; Joel 2:13; Hosea 14:1; Nehemiah 1:9; Job 22:23a (NIV); Jeremiah 24:7; Lamentations 3:40; Isaiah 55:7; Deuteronomy 4:30; James 4:8 (NLT)

1) Do you want more than you've been given?

2) Are you ungrateful, selfish, or driven?

3) Do you ever choose the cold instead of the warmth of His protected fold?

Open My Eyes

2 Kings 6:15-17; 2 Corinthians 4:18; 2 Corinthians 10:3-5; 1 John 5:4; Isaiah 41:10-12; Psalm 56:3; Psalm 93:4; 1 Corinthians 2:5; Jeremiah 32:27

1) How can you pray for eyes to see the spiritual forces at battle for your loved one?

2) When do you most need the reminder that there are more with you than with the enemy?

3) How can you fight against the misperception that God has surrendered His authority?

Proving Ground

Genesis 32:24-26; Exodus 21:6; Isaiah 48:10; Zechariah 13:9; Proverbs 17:3; Deuteronomy 8:2-5; 1 Peter 1:6-7; Job 23:10

1) How has God shown His faithfulness, constancy, and dependability during your struggle?

2) How has He proven Himself reliable, trustworthy, and steadfast?

3) Do you have a limp that reminds you of your reliance and dependence on God?

4) What scars do you bear that show you belong to Jesus?

Not by Chance

Matthew 10:29-31; Isaiah 45:7, 9; Job 42:2; Romans 9:21;
Exodus 4:11; Psalm 139:16

1) In what ways do you feel responsible for your child's rebellion?

2) Are there familial patterns or genetic predispositions at play?

3) How can you thank God for both the straight and crooked paths
in your life?

Prodigal Testimony

Hebrews 4:16; Romans 11:6; 1 Peter 5:10; Ephesians 1:7; Titus 2:11-
12a; Luke 8:39; Titus 3:3-7; 1 Timothy 1:13-16; Proverbs 4:14-19

1) When did you first notice your child's steps were veering into the
wilderness of enemy territory?

2) How does a prodigal's departure and return demonstrate to
others the testimony of the gospel of the grace of God?

3) Do you view your circumstances as a trial to endure or an
opportunity for testimony?

May Our Prodigal Story Make Us Run to You

Ephesians 2:4-5, 8; Acts 4:12; Romans 10:9; Acts 16:31; 2
Corinthians 3:5; 2 Corinthians 4:7; 2 Corinthians 7:10; 1 John 1:9;
Acts 3:19; 1 Corinthians 15:22; 2 Corinthians 12:9; Hebrews 7:25

1) Has your prodigal's wandering brought you to the end of yourself yet?

2) How has God sustained you and answered desperate prayers for your children?

Surrendered

Philippians 2:13; Matthew 16:24-25; Matthew 19:29; Romans 12:1; Isaiah 64:8; Mark 8:35; Psalm 116:12 (NIV); Psalm 127:1, 3-5; Proverbs 16:3; James 1:17

1) What do you need to surrender back to God?

2) What value has God imbued in your life experience?

The Gift of Prodigal Parenting

2 Peter 3:9; Romans 15:5, 15; Acts 1:8; Ephesians 1:17-20; Ephesians 3:16-20; Psalm 103:13; Psalm 145:8-9; John 3:16; Hebrews 9:12, 14; Matthew 20:28; Philippians 2:6-8; 1 Peter 3:18; Hebrews 12:2

1) How has your prodigal child's journey brought blessing into your life?

2) How does it reveal attributes of God you might not otherwise perceive?

3) How can you remind yourself of the gift in the grief, the privilege in the path?

Conveying Comfort

1 Peter 1:6; 1 Peter 4:10, 12-13; 1 Peter 5:10; Romans 8:17-18; Acts 14:22; 2 Corinthians 4:17; Ephesians 3:13; Hebrews 12:11; Galatians 6:2; Philippians 2:4

1) How have these words provided comfort on your journey?

2) Do you feel a sense of community on an intensely isolating path?

3) How could you comfort others with the comfort you have received?

ACKNOWLEDGEMENTS

These prayer poems are all addressed to the One who made possible the words and the experiences behind the words. I thank God for carrying me into and through this wilderness. I thank my prodigal son for permitting me to share my perspective on this journey and showing me grace as I attempt to parent him in God-honoring ways. Plus, I thank him for the trials we tread together because they grow and stretch my faith. It is my deepest prayer that his path will lead to exponential growth for him, for me, and for any readers who consider these poems.

I wish to thank the early readers who graciously provided feedback: Lynn Suchy, Karin Trauman, Carol Wurtz, Linda Himes, Bobbie Scott, Karen Pommier, Leti Crowell, Nanette Helm, Paul du Plessis, Sarah Suzanne Noble, and Kyle L. White. I also wish to thank my writing circle, Westside Wordsmiths, for critiquing a few of the poems.

Finally, special gratitude to my mother, whose encouragement always kept me writing. While dementia steals from her the ability to fully appreciate my words now, she deserves credit for her literary, emotional, and spiritual support.